967.62
Ken   Kenya in pictures

	DATE DUE	
Green (far)		
AUG 3 1989		
MAY 7 1990		

KENYA

...in Pictures

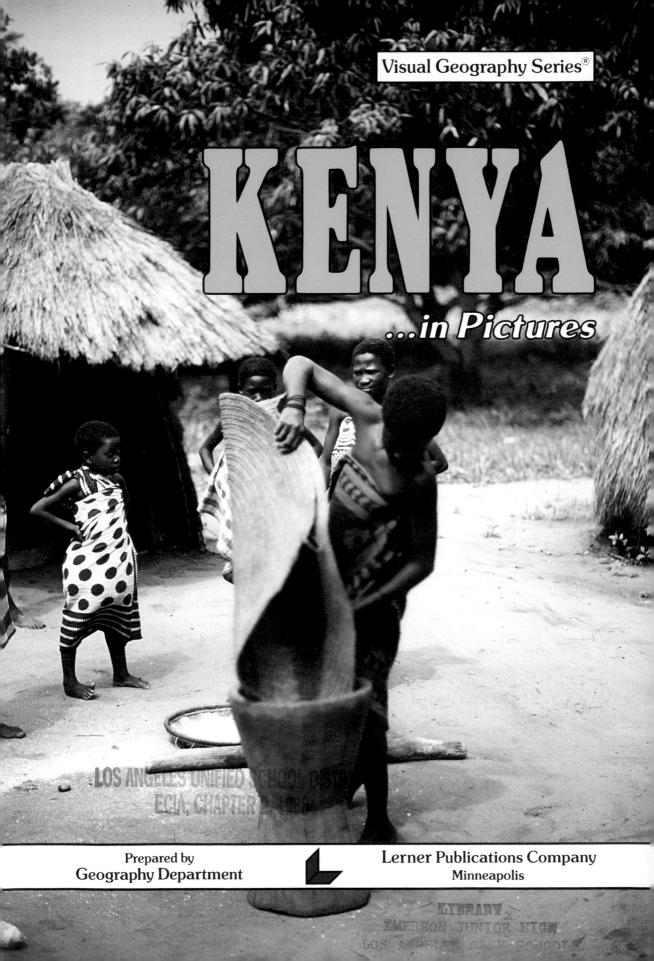

Visual Geography Series®

KENYA
...in Pictures

Prepared by
Geography Department

Lerner Publications Company
Minneapolis

APR   1989

9.00

Copyright © 1988 by Lerner Publications Company

VISUAL GEOGRAPHY SERIES®

Publisher
Harry Jonas Lerner
Associate Publisher
Nancy M. Campbell
Senior Editor
Mary M. Rodgers
Editor
Gretchen Bratvold
Editorial Assistant
Nora W. Kniskern
Illustrations Editor
Karen A. Sirvaitis
Consultants/Contributors
Thomas O'Toole
Sandra K. Davis
Designer
Jim Simondet
Cartographer
Carol F. Barrett
Indexer
Sylvia Timian
Production Manager
Richard J. Hannah

Independent Picture Service

A student works at a machine in an engineering lab-
oratory.

This is an all-new edition of the Visual Geography
Series. Previous editions have been published by
Sterling Publishing Company, New York City, and
some of the original textual information has been re-
tained. New photographs, maps, charts, captions, and
updated information have been added. The text has
been entirely reset in 10/12 Century Textbook.

LIBRARY OF CONGRESS CATALOGING-IN-PUBLICATION DATA

Kenya in pictures.

(Visual geography series)
Rev. ed. of: Kenya in pictures / prepared by Joel
Reuben.
Includes index.
Summary: Text and photographs introduce the
geography, history, government, people, and economy
of the thirty-fourth African nation to gain independence.
1. Kenya. [1. Kenya] I. Reuben, Joel. Kenya in pic-
tures. II. Lerner Publications Company. Geography
Dept. III. Series: Visual geography series (Minneapolis,
Minn.)
DT433.522.K464   1988   967.6'2   87–1761
ISBN 0-8225-1830-9 (lib. bdg.)

International Standard Book Number: 0-8225-1830-9
Library of Congress Catalog Card Number: 87-17261

Independent Picture Service

Uhuru Highway near Nairobi features British-style round-
abouts to guide traffic through intersections.

Acknowledgments

Title page photo courtesy of Sarah J. Hausauer.

Elevation contours adapted from *The Times Atlas of
the World*, seventh comprehensive edition (New York:
Times Books, 1985).

2 3 4 5 6 7 8 9 10 97 96 95 94 93 92 91 90 89

Steamers on Lake Victoria make stops in Kenya, Tanzania, and Uganda. In addition to carrying people, the boats transport mail, agricultural products, and even automobiles.

Contents

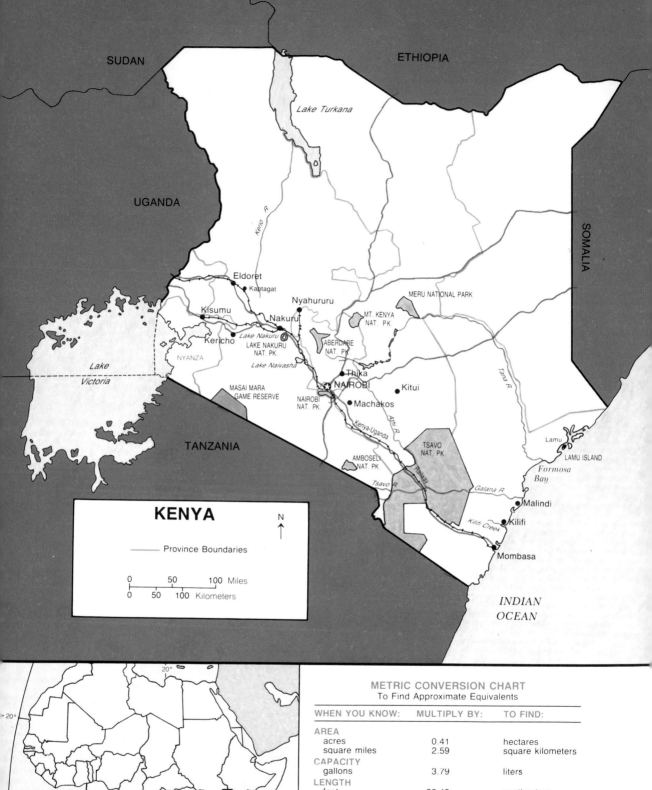

SUDAN

ETHIOPIA

Lake Turkana

UGANDA

Kerio R.

SOMALIA

Eldoret
• Kaptagat

Nyahururu

MERU NATIONAL PARK

MT. KENYA
NAT. PK.

Kisumu

Nakuru

Lake Nakuru

KERICHO

Lake Nakuru
LAKE NAKURU
NAT. PK.

ABERDARE
NAT. PK.

Kericho

NYANZA

Lake Naivasha

Tana R.

Thika

*Lake
Victoria*

NAIROBI

• Kitui

MASAI MARA
GAME RESERVE

NAIROBI
NAT. PK.

• Machakos

Kenya-Uganda

Athi R.

TANZANIA

AMBOSELI
NAT. PK.

TSAVO
NAT. PK.

Lamu

LAMU ISLAND

*Formosa
Bay*

Tsavo R.

Railway

Galana R.

• Malindi

Kilifi Creek

• Kilifi

Mombasa

KENYA

N
↑

—— Province Boundaries

0   50   100 Miles
0   50   100 Kilometers

INDIAN
OCEAN

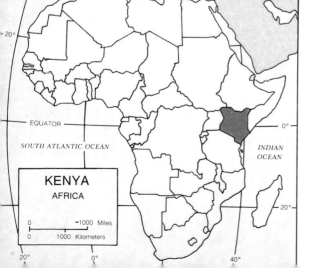

20°

20°

EQUATOR

SOUTH ATLANTIC OCEAN

0°

INDIAN
OCEAN

KENYA
AFRICA

1000 Miles
0   1000 Kilometers

20°   0°   40°

METRIC CONVERSION CHART
To Find Approximate Equivalents

WHEN YOU KNOW:	MULTIPLY BY:	TO FIND:
AREA		
acres	0.41	hectares
square miles	2.59	square kilometers
CAPACITY		
gallons	3.79	liters
LENGTH		
feet	30.48	centimeters
yards	0.91	meters
miles	1.61	kilometers
MASS (weight)		
pounds	0.45	kilograms
tons	0.91	metric tons
VOLUME		
cubic yards	0.77	cubic meters
TEMPERATURE		
degrees Fahrenheit	0.56 (*after* subtracting 32)	degrees Celsius

Keiyo dancers in brightly colored clothes celebrate at a festival in Kitany.

Introduction

The Republic of Kenya became Africa's thirty-fourth independent nation on December 12, 1963, and the people of Kenya rejoiced at the conclusion of 68 years of colonial rule. After achieving independence, Kenya was faced with many problems, which it shared with other emerging countries. Nigeria and Ghana—two of Africa's most influential nations—were both dangerously close to civil war as a result of ethnic conflicts and inexperienced leadership. The international community watched to see whether Kenyans could overcome similar problems to achieve stability and interethnic cooperation.

Thus far, Kenya has successfully avoided major ethnic conflicts and has maintained a relatively efficient administrative system. Living standards, education, health, housing, and economic activity have all improved, and the nation has become a respected voice in the United Nations as well as in the African community.

Kenya's motto, *harambee*—Kiswahili (also known as Swahili) for "pull together"—symbolizes the efforts of all of the country's ethnic groups to unify and stabilize the nation. These efforts have resulted in better health care facilities, improvements in education, and a stable society.

Able to survive intense heat and drought, acacia trees shade the arid Kenyan plains, as well as other parts of Africa and Australia. Some types of acacias yield economically important products, such as edible seeds, timber, and gum.

1) The Land

Kenya is located on the eastern side of the continent of Africa, exactly on the equator. Bounded on the southeast by the Indian Ocean, Kenya shares borders with Tanzania to the south, Uganda to the west, Sudan to the northwest, Ethiopia to the north, and Somalia to the northeast. With a total area of 224,960 square miles, Kenya is slightly smaller than the state of Texas.

Most of the land—roughly the northern three-fifths of the country—is desertlike and unable to sustain a large population. In contrast, the southern two-fifths of Kenya has a mild climate and receives plentiful rainfall. Home to 85 percent of Kenya's people, this area also generates nearly all the economic activity that takes place in the country.

Topography

Kenya has four distinct geographical regions. One region, the southeastern coast, fronts on the Indian Ocean at sea level. Moving inland and north, the land gradually rises in elevation up to the capital city of Nairobi, approximately 300 miles from the coast. A second region encompasses the land surrounding Nairobi and reaches a plateau averaging nearly 5,000 feet in height. A third area is the arid northern region above the equator, which ranges from 500 feet above sea level on its eastern side to 5,000 feet on its western side.

Kenya's fourth topographical region, which lies in the southwest, comprises a highland plateau broken up by two mountain ranges—the Aberdare Mountains and the Mau Escarpment. These two mountain ranges run north to south through west central Kenya and average 10,000 to 11,000 feet in elevation. Running between the Aberdares and the Mau Escarpment, the Rift Valley separates the cliffs formed by the two ranges.

The Rift Valley in Kenya is part of the Great Rift Valley. It begins in southwest Asia and cuts its way across the African continent through Kenya's western highlands and south to Mozambique. Formed by volcanic action, the Great Rift Valley is a channel of land whose floor varies in altitude. Within Kenya the floor is quite high in elevation, rising to over 6,000 feet above sea level at Lake Naivasha.

Courtesy of Sarah J. Hausauer

Named for nineteenth-century Scottish explorer Joseph Thomson, thomson's gazelle is the smallest of the gazelles. It roams Kenya's high plains, feeding on grasses.

Courtesy of Stephen Mustoe

Mount Kenya, an extinct volcano in central Kenya, is the second highest mountain in Africa after Tanzania's Kilimanjaro.

Located in the center of Kenya just south of the equator, Mount Kenya is the highest peak in the country. With an altitude of 17,058 feet, this extinct volcano is the second highest mountain on the African continent after Mount Kilimanjaro in Tanzania. Another prominent peak, Mount Elgon (14,178 feet), lies on Kenya's western border with Uganda.

Rivers and Lakes

Kenya has three water drainage systems —the coastal lowlands where rivers drain into the Indian Ocean, the Rift Valley system where streams feed into a chain of lakes within the valley, and a group of small streams to the west of the Rift Valley that flow into Lake Victoria. The chief rivers flow through the coastal lowlands in south central and southeastern Kenya.

Beginning its 440-mile course on the eastern edge of the Rift Valley, the Tana River is the longest river in Kenya. The Tana wanders southward and eastward, becoming navigable about 150 miles from Formosa Bay, where it empties into the Indian Ocean. The 340-mile-long Galana River is formed by the merging of two waterways, the Athi from central Kenya and the Tsavo from southern Kenya near Tanzania. Several miles north of the seaport town of Malindi, the Galana River empties into the Indian Ocean.

In addition to rivers, several lakes water Kenya. Two of Africa's great lakes—Victoria and Turkana—cross Kenya's borders. Gigantic Lake Victoria, part of which lies in Kenya's southwestern corner, is the world's second largest freshwater body. Only North America's Lake Superior is bigger. Lake Turkana lies almost entirely

An Egyptian ibis—considered sacred by ancient peoples—flies over Lake Naivasha, which is the largest of the five lakes on the floor of the Rift Valley.

A waterfall gushes over a sheer drop at Nyahururu, northwest of Nairobi in Kenya's Rift Valley.

Passengers on a ferry work together to transport themselves across Kilifi Creek. As they pull on ropes, the workers move the platform on which they stand across the water.

A public bus, or *matatu,* is mired in the mud near Kaptagat. Because only 12 percent of Kenya's roads are paved, the rainy season often has a great impact on transportation.

Courtesy of Stephen Mustoe

within northern Kenya, except for a small part of its northern shore, which pushes into Ethiopia.

Five bodies of water make up a chain of lesser lakes on the floor of the Rift Valley. About 40 miles northwest of Nairobi lies Lake Naivasha, the largest in the chain—a beautiful lake with striking, clear-blue waters.

Climate

Although Kenya straddles the equator, high altitudes in the central and western portions of the country temper the climate. Along the coast, the temperature averages 80° F, but near Nairobi the average ranges from 57° F to 70° F, depending on the time of day. Significant temperature changes occur between afternoon and evening, but the climate varies more in terms of rainfall than temperature.

Kenya has two rainy seasons separated by two dry periods. Because Kenya is mainly an agricultural nation, its rains are of utmost importance to the economy. The two rainy seasons are the long rains from April to June and the short rains from October to December. During the remaining months, Kenya is dry but may have occasional shower activity. January, February, August, and September are the driest months.

Although each rainy season lasts for about three months, more rain falls continuously during the long rains. These

Courtesy of Sarah J. Hausauer

White sand beaches north of Mombasa line the shores of the Indian Ocean and are sometimes the site of violent monsoons.

12

rainy seasons are quite regular and, while they last, rain falls from one to four hours daily. The northern regions above the equator hardly receive any rain at all, but the coastal, central, and western parts of the country receive over 40 inches of rain per year.

Flora

Literally thousands of flowers—both wild and cultivated—grow in the southern two-thirds of Kenya. Plant life on the coast is tropical, diverse, and lush. Coconut palms and dense mangrove forests, as well as teak and sandalwood trees, fringe the coast of the Indian Ocean. Inland, the coastal vegetation thins out to thorny scrub, along with occasional acacia (flowering thorn trees) and baobab (broad-trunked trees with edible fruit). This zone of scrubby vegetation broadens as it merges with the semidesert region bordering on Somalia to the northeast.

Courtesy of Sarah J. Hausauer

From the observation tower at Lake Nakuru National Park, visitors can see hippopotamuses, flamingos, marabou storks, cormorants, and other park inhabitants.

Courtesy of Stephen Mustoe

The coconut palm produces an oil whose lubricating qualities were a boon to British industrialists in the nineteenth century. The tree is also harvested for its coconuts, whose husks are made into strong fiber.

At interior elevations of 3,000 feet or more, broad grasslands cover the land and acacia groves line the river banks. Areas receiving the most rainfall often sprout groves of giant bamboo. In the south central highlands around Nairobi, some flowering trees can be found. Among them is the jacaranda, a tall tree that has showy, purple-blue blossoms in the springtime. Flowers and shrubs in this region grow in a splendid range of sizes, shapes, and colors. Bougainvillea, for example—with its many-shaded blossoms of purple, red, orange, or white—can grow to be 16 feet high.

To the west at higher altitudes, impressive giant lobelias and groundsels are common. Dense forests with pines and deciduous trees (which shed their leaves each year) appear as the land rises beyond 6,000 feet.

13

Independent Picture Service

Fauna

The wildlife of Kenya is among the most abundant and varied in the world, and several large game parks have been established so that wildlife enthusiasts can observe animals in their natural habitats. Large animals such as elephants, giraffes, buffalo, and rhinoceroses roam the high plains in sizable numbers, as do zebras and several kinds of antelope—impalas, wildebeests, hartebeests, and gazelles. Here, too, are beasts of prey—lions, cheetahs, leopards, hyenas, jackals, and wild dogs. Smaller animals, such as tree hyraxes and monkeys, inhabit both the highland plains and forest lands farther southwest.

Horned buffalo roam the high plains in herds of up to a thousand animals, grazing in the early morning and evening and resting in the heat of midday.

Independent Picture Service

Lazy as crocodiles may seem, they can move like lightning when necessary. They are hunted—sometimes illegally in national parks—for their valuable hides.

The leopard can serve to regulate the population of other animals. For example, in some areas baboons are a nuisance to livestock farmers, who resist hunting leopards in the hope that the cats will attack the baboons. In other locales, however, leopards have been hunted almost to extinction.

Independent Picture Service

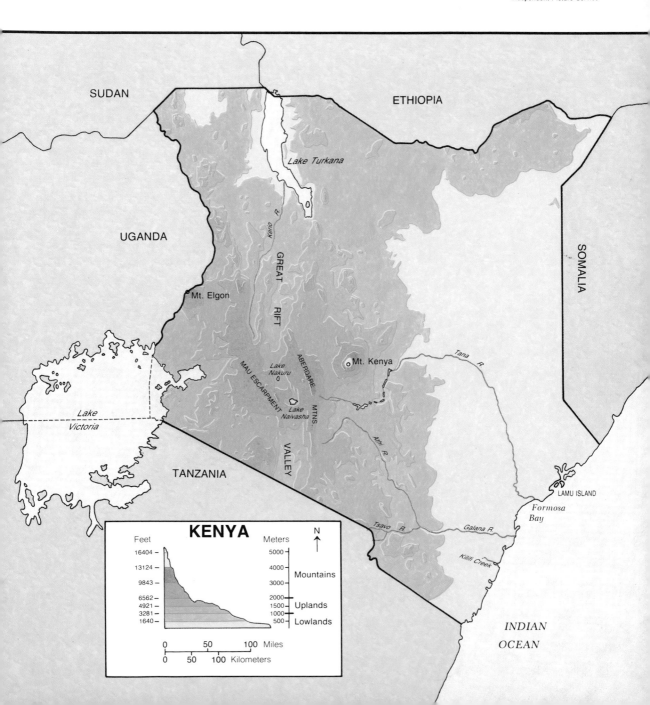

KENYA

Feet		Meters	
16404 —		5000 —	
13124 —		4000 —	Mountains
9843 —		3000 —	
6562 —		2000 —	
4921 —		1500 —	Uplands
3281 —		1000 —	
1640 —		500 —	Lowlands

| 0 | 50 | 100 | Miles |
| 0 | 50 | 100 | Kilometers |

In a rare moment out of the water, this hippopotamus grazes at Mzima Springs in Tsavo National Park, one of the largest parks in Kenya.

Independent Picture Service

Courtesy of Stephen Mustoe

Zebras' stripes serve as camouflage—a protective coloration to help the animals visually blend into their surroundings. Hunters have drastically reduced the zebra population in all areas of Africa.

Photo by Phil Porter

Courtesy of Sarah J. Hausauer

An orphaned baby rhinoceros at the zoo in Nairobi National Park eats lunch.

Birds common to the highlands include ostriches, eagles, kites, and vultures. Lakeshores and coastal waters swarm with pelicans, cranes, ibis, storks, egrets, and flamingos. Throughout the southern two-thirds of the country a variety of brightly colored parakeets, parrots, and songbirds are found.

Many kinds of reptiles are plentiful in Kenya. Sizes range from small salamanders to sizable crocodiles. Although some reptiles are large or poisonous, in general they are unaggressive and avoid people. The largest of more than 100 species of snakes is the gigantic but nonpoisonous python. Many smaller snakes—puff adders, vipers, mambas, and cobras—are deadly. Insects such as mosquitoes, bees, and flies often carry diseases, which threaten both humans and animals.

The tilapia and Nile perch thrive in Kenya's lakes and streams. Trout, which have been introduced into the cool waters of the Aberdare Mountains, provide sport for local fishermen. Kenya's coastal waters are

17

one's needs. Neither enough jobs nor enough good-quality, low-cost homes exist for the new residents. These strains on urban resources are somewhat reduced in Kenya, because it has a number of important manufacturing towns—Mombasa, Eldoret, Nakuru, and Thika—besides its chief industrial center and capital city, Nairobi.

NAIROBI

Nairobi has grown to a metropolis of about 1.1 million people since its founding in 1899. Life in the capital is fast paced, and a visitor would find little difference between living in Nairobi and living in any other large urban area. A mixture of both Eastern and Western cultures, Nairobi is frequented by Africans, Asians, and Europeans, making it a truly international city.

Courtesy of Stephen Mustoe

The Kenyatta International Conference Center helps to shape Nairobi's distinctive skyline.

home to large tropical fish—marlin, sailfish, sharks, yellowfin tuna, barracuda, and dorado.

Cities

Many Kenyans in search of jobs and better living conditions are moving from rural areas into large cities. Consequently, like cities in many African countries, Kenya's urban areas face the problem of a population that is growing so fast that the cities' resources cannot meet every-

Courtesy of Sarah J. Hausauer

Bunting along the roofs of a Mombasa market street features the colors of the Kenyan flag. The decorations are in honor of the annual East African Safari Rally, a national auto race.

18

Nairobi's population is growing by 8 percent annually—twice the national rate, which is one of the highest in the world. At least one-third of the city's estimated 1.1 million people live in shantytowns, which sharply contrast with this attractive skyline.

Nairobi is one of Africa's most beautiful and productive cities, rivaling Cairo in Egypt and Johannesburg in South Africa as a busy road, rail, and air hub. National and international organizations based in Nairobi influence events on the entire African continent. Most Kenyan government buildings are located in Nairobi, including those that house the Kenyan legislature and all of the ministries.

SECONDARY CITIES

In contrast to Nairobi, Mombasa—Kenya's leading port on the Indian Ocean—is a very old settlement. The first Arab traders probably lived in Mombasa during the eleventh century. Much smaller than Nairobi, Mombasa has a population of 425,000. Perhaps because of its size and its warm climate, Mombasa has a slower pace of life than does Nairobi. A large Arabic population and many buildings modeled on Eastern architecture contribute to an atmosphere in Mombasa that is quite different from the European flavor of Nairobi. Because of its excellent beaches on the Indian Ocean, Mombasa is also Kenya's chief resort city.

Automobiles are prohibited on the island of Lamu, where narrow, twisting streets that are impassable by car reveal the Arabic origins of the city of Lamu.

Most of Kenya's cities developed because of their nearness to a trade route or to land suited to a certain crop. For example, Kericho (population 32,800) began as a trading town to serve the large tea-growing estates in the region. People still come to Kericho to work on the tea estates.

Two other cities that owe their importance to their location are Nakuru (population 93,000) and Kisumu (population 153,000). Founded as a trading post in the heart of the Rift Valley, Nakuru is situated on a natural route between western Kenya and Nairobi. Kisumu, on Lake Victoria, became a rail center for products from Mombasa destined for Uganda, northern Tanzania, and Zaire. Surrounded by good farmland and fine grazing land, Kisumu became a meeting place for traders of crops and cattle.

A vendor in traditional clothing sells coffee to passersby on a Mombasa street corner. Large numbers of vendors participate in informal economies without keeping actual shops or records of their business activities.

The National Archives in Nairobi house historic and government documents, but the diversity of the capital's architecture and ethnic groups testifies more completely to Kenya's rich history.

2) History and Government

Archaeologists have uncovered bones and tools of early peoples throughout Kenya, but the majority of the finds have come from the Rift Valley region. Few facts are known about these early humans and their cultures, but their tools and fossil remains have convinced historians that people lived in East Africa as early as two million years ago.

Arabs made the first outside contacts with Kenya's inhabitants about 2,000 years ago. About 500 years later, Greeks, Romans, Persians, and East Indians began trading with the people who lived along Kenya's coast. The traders recorded information about the best time of the year to travel on the Indian Ocean and told of the ivory and spices they had obtained

21

Courtesy of Sarah J. Hausauer

Muslim women shop at a market on the island of Lamu. Their black gowns, called *buibuis,* are reminders of Islam's presence in Kenya since the tenth century.

from the interior. These foreigners did not venture far into Kenya from the coast of the Indian Ocean. Although the merchants knew people existed in the interior, they did not attempt to meet them.

Early History

At nearly the same time as this early trading on the coast of Kenya, large migrations were taking place on the African continent. About 2,000 years ago some of

Courtesy of Sarah J. Hausauer

These abandoned shelters, which stand about four feet high, were made from reeds. Begun thousands of years ago, this traditional form of housing is still used by the Masai people.

these peoples began moving eastward and southward from their homelands on the borders of modern Nigeria and Cameroon. Forced out of their own territories, in part by a population increase, these people came to the region of present-day Kenya seeking fertile farmland. The newcomers, who spoke languages that evolved into the widespread Bantu language family, firmly established themselves in Kenya by about A.D. 900.

Immigration of Bantu-speaking peoples into Kenya increased until it reached its peak in the fourteenth and fifteenth centuries. During the four to five centuries of Bantu movement, other groups also were migrating. Nilotic peoples (who had originally lived in the Nile River Valley) came from Sudan and southern Egypt. Cushitic peoples came from present-day Somalia, from northern Africa, and from the eastern coast. All of these groups encountered the Bantu-speaking peoples in the course of their travels. Kenya was the crossroads for all of these movements, which accounts for the mosaic of ethnic groups and languages in Kenya today.

While the Bantu and other groups pushed into Kenya from the north, another force—the Islamic religion—was becoming influential on the eastern coast of Africa. Traders from southwest Asia introduced

Islam – the Muslim religion founded by the prophet Muhammad – into this region by the late sixth century.

The death of Muhammad in A.D. 632 and the growth of the Muslim religion between the seventh and tenth centuries indirectly caused the Arab world to take an interest in Kenya. As the Muslim religion spread in southwest Asia, quarreling arose between those who followed the teachings of Muhammad and those who did not. Many people left the region, in part because of increased population pressures and wars that erupted on the Arabian Peninsula. Escaping by boat, these people were carried by the monsoons (strong, seasonal winds) across the Indian Ocean to East Africa, where they settled along the Kenyan coast.

By the ninth century various Islamic groups controlled most of Kenya's coastal area through trade, and by the eleventh century they had established settlements. With the strength of their efficient trade and new religion, the Arabs dominated the coast of present-day Kenya for nearly 500 years, until a new group of foreigners— the Portuguese—arrived.

Courtesy of Stephen Mustoe

Nairobi's Jamia Mosque recalls a time when Arabs dominated commerce and introduced Islamic beliefs. In the 1980s only 6 percent of Kenya's population was Muslim.

Although the Portuguese stayed in East Africa for about 200 years, their most permanent legacy is the fortress of Fort Jesus *(left)*. Portuguese explorers encountered the prosperous Arab culture on Kenya's coast in the late fifteenth century. They destroyed Muslim settlements in their search for gold and spices, but in subsequent years they turned their interest to the New World and the East Indies.

Coastal Influences

The Portuguese began to explore the coasts of Africa in the early fifteenth century in search of gold and spices. By 1444 they had become seriously interested in Africa, and in 1498 Vasco da Gama led an expedition around the southern tip of the continent (later named the Cape of Good Hope) and up the eastern coast toward Kenya. Finding the prosperous coastal culture of the Arabs, the Portuguese destroyed many Muslim settlements as they searched for gold and spices and fought to gain control of the area. The Portuguese won control of the Kenyan coast by the early 1500s and used the area as a trading base for approximately 200 years.

Because Portugal did not find the commodities it wanted in East Africa, Portuguese interest turned to other regions. For about the next 150 years, Arabs governed Kenya's profitable coastal trade from the island of Zanzibar off the southeastern tip of Kenya's coast. Neither the Muslims of the coast nor the Portuguese, however, greatly influenced the Bantu-speakers and other peoples in Kenya's interior. With permission from the sultan of Zanzibar, European missionaries began to explore Kenya's interior in 1850.

Interior Exploration

Before 1850 European knowledge of East Africa had been limited to the coastal areas. Between 1850 and 1870, however, the search for markets and raw materials led to an interest in the inland areas. Along with the missionary activity in Kenya, several new European intrusions into the region occurred during this period. Motivation for exploration was political as well as economic; concerned about French and German influence in Africa, Great Britain took an interest in East Africa.

Seeking the sources of the Nile and Niger rivers, as well as knowledge about the vegetation and wildlife of Africa, the British ventured into the Kenya-Uganda region of East Africa. With financial support from the British government, John Speke and James Grant explored the area around Lake Victoria and the Rift Valley. Their discovery of the source of the Nile River in what is now Uganda became a crucial factor in the development of British interest in the Kenya-Uganda area.

Germany also explored East Africa during this period. The journeys of two German missionaries—Johann Krapf and Johannes Rebmann—in the mid-nineteenth century resulted in the first European contact with the people of the Mount Kenya region. Both German and British exploration in East Africa continued, which caused competition between the two countries. European historians have called this period of accelerated exploration and territorial acquisition, which began in the 1880s, the "scramble for Africa."

Independent Picture Service

Aimed at the waters of the Indian Ocean, this cannon has remained silent at Fort Jesus for nearly 300 years. The Portuguese built the fort in Mombasa in 1593 but abandoned it in 1700 when Arabs again gained control of the East African coast.

A welcoming committee composed of both African workers and colonial officials awaits the arrival in 1907 of Winston Churchill—who would later become one of Britain's most popular prime ministers.

British Control

Very little of the African continent was actually controlled by Europeans before the 1880s. Unlike Portugal, Britain and France secured areas of influence for trade and missionary activity, but they did not establish colonies. Between 1880 and 1900 this situation changed dramatically, and European governments gained control over 40 of the 46 political units into which Africa had been divided.

This division of the continent took place at the Berlin Conference in 1885, which was attended by Great Britain, France, Germany, and Belgium. Each nation presented claims to various parts of the African continent, and together they formulated rules for colonization. Even as the conference was being prepared, Germany was strengthening its position in East Africa by quietly signing treaties with African leaders in the area.

East Africa—including what is now Kenya—was partitioned between the British and the Germans, with all land north of the middle of Lake Victoria claimed by the

In 1913 this road in Nairobi was little more than pebbles and sand, or *murram.* The city's growth was aided by its central position in the path of the Kenya-Uganda Railroad as the line pushed its way inland.

British and with everything south of this line under German control. Kenya, however, was largely ignored by the British, who were much more concerned with Uganda and the headwaters of the Nile River. Britain feared that if it did not control Uganda, another European power might take over the area and dam up the Nile River at its source.

Once the British were established in Uganda, Kenya became important as Uganda's link to the sea. In 1896 the British took their first major step in Kenya's development. At that time the British Parliament allotted funds for the building of the Kenya-Uganda Railroad to link the historic port of Mombasa with Uganda and the Nile region. Work began in 1896 and, despite numerous hardships, the new railway line reached Nairobi—300 miles from Mombasa—in 1899. By 1901 the line stretched roughly 500 miles from Mombasa to Lake Victoria. A few years later it reached Uganda.

The British transported thousands of East Indians to work on the railway, believing that they would be easier to control than the local African population. Remaining in Kenya upon the completion of the railway, many East Indians opened small stores, became businesspeople, or continued as employees of the railway. They did not become landowners, however, because the British government did

Photo by Phil Porter

The British government's first major development effort in Kenya was to build a railway from the coast at Mombasa to Lake Victoria at the turn of the twentieth century. Today Kenya is served by the Kenya Railways Corporation, which operates about 1,300 miles of railroad—including the original Kenya-Uganda route.

Wood-framed churches, such as this Catholic one in Kapkoi north of Kisumu, began to appear in the nineteenth century. A variety of U.S. and European missionary groups worked in Africa throughout the colonial era.

Courtesy of Stephen Mustoe

not allow nonwhites to purchase or farm land in the British territory—known as the East Africa Protectorate.

Although occupation of Kenya was not foremost in the minds of the politicians recommending the railway, the British government gave and sold choice land in Kenya to European settlers in order to make the railroad profitable. The offer did not attract an impressive number of colonists, but those who did come planted large tracts of land and became quite wealthy.

Seeds of Conflict

Among the many problems encountered by the East Africa Protectorate were disagreements between the settlers and the colonial administration. To give the newcomers some responsibility in running the protectorate, the British established the Legislative Council in 1905. By the end of World War I, the 9,000 Europeans in Kenya exercised their representative voice in the government through the Legislative Council.

The black population, however, had no political power in the protectorate. Although the British government officially claimed to be concerned with the rights of the blacks, the government allotted the choicest lands to the white minority and forced the blacks to relocate on less fertile areas that had been set aside for them.

Independent Picture Service

Farming is often a family's main source of food and income, and land is held in high esteem. The British land seizures in the late 1800s disrupted the culture of the Kikuyu, who used specific land plots, or *githakas*, to bind individuals to the larger group.

28

In addition, the Europeans discouraged blacks and Asians from farming for themselves, hiring them instead to work on the large, European-owned estates.

The Twentieth Century

During World War I, Germany—Britain's enemy on the continent of Europe and rival on the continent of Africa—raided and harassed the British in East Africa. When the war ended in 1918, the Germans lost their Tanganyika colony south of Kenya, and the British added it to their Kenya-Uganda possessions.

World War I had important effects on Kenya. Many settlers had been called to serve in the British army, and the export economy was hurt by their absence. The white population of Kenya increased after the war, however, as former soldiers were given land to settle in the protectorate. By changing the status and name of the East Africa Protectorate to the Kenya Colony and Protectorate in 1920, Great Britain officially proclaimed Kenya as part of its empire.

During the period between World War I and World War II, significant political forces were at work in Kenya. In the early

At the turn of the twentieth century, the colonial government imposed head taxes on villages that were near colonial settlements. Many Africans were required to work in European-owned fields in order to pay the tax.

Independent Picture Service

Independent Picture Service

Built in 1935, the Nairobi Law Courts house the judicial branch of the government. An African became Kenya's chief justice in 1968, ending white domination of the justice system.

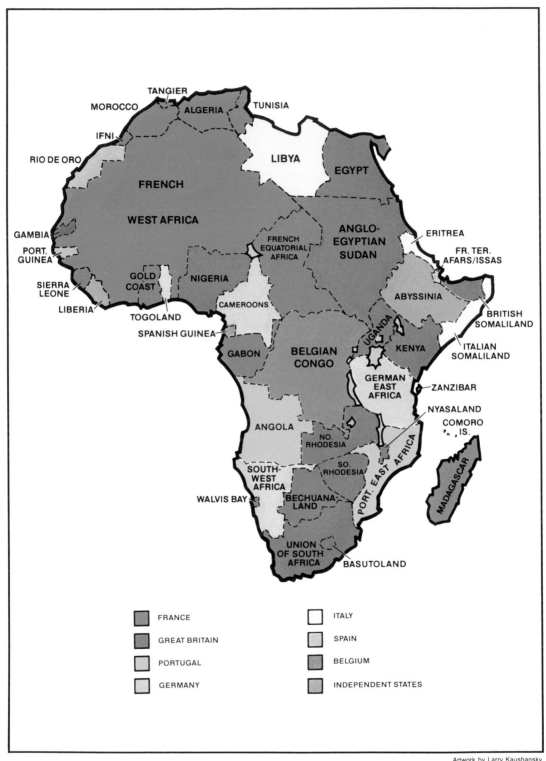

TANGIER

MOROCCO

ALGERIA

TUNISIA

IFNI

RIO DE ORO

LIBYA

EGYPT

FRENCH

WEST AFRICA

ANGLO-
EGYPTIAN
SUDAN

ERITREA

FR. TER.
AFARS/ISSAS

GAMBIA

PORT.
GUINEA

FRENCH
EQUATORIAL
AFRICA

SIERRA
LEONE

GOLD
COAST

NIGERIA

ABYSSINIA

LIBERIA

CAMEROONS

BRITISH
SOMALILAND

TOGOLAND

SPANISH GUINEA

UGANDA

KENYA

ITALIAN
SOMALILAND

GABON

BELGIAN
CONGO

GERMAN
EAST
AFRICA

ZANZIBAR

NYASALAND

ANGOLA

NO.
RHODESIA

COMORO
IS.

SOUTH-
WEST
AFRICA

SO.
RHODESIA

PORT. EAST AFRICA

MADAGASCAR

WALVIS BAY

BECHUANA-
LAND

UNION
OF SOUTH
AFRICA

BASUTOLAND

	FRANCE		ITALY
	GREAT BRITAIN		SPAIN
	PORTUGAL		BELGIUM
	GERMANY		INDEPENDENT STATES

By the late nineteenth century, the Europeans had carved the continent of Africa into areas of influence. Present-day Kenya was a British colony until 1963. Map information taken from *The Anchor Atlas of World History,* 1978.

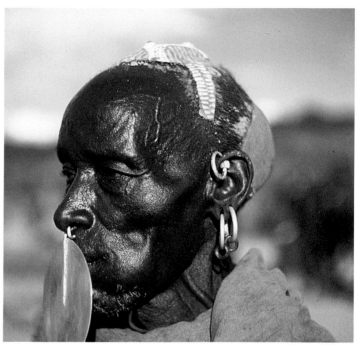

An old Pokot man is a respected figure in his community. Under colonial rule, the British did not replace local leaders, but rather integrated them into the lowest level of the administrative structure.

1920s the Asian population raised the issue of representation in the colonial administration. Asians, who far outnumbered white settlers, wanted voting rights and representation on the Legislative Council. Europeans resisted the demand, and the issue was taken to Great Britain. Fearing that violence in the colony would increase financial costs for the military and police, the British government permitted Asians to have five representatives on the council.

The Rise of Kenyan Nationalism

Perhaps the most important development of the period between the two world wars was the emergence of black Kenyans as a political force. Pushed off their land, many Kenyans, especially those of the Kikuyu ethnic group, took jobs in urban areas such as Nairobi and Nakuru. City life, however, was also difficult because of rising taxes, falling wages, and the introduction of hated black identification passes— which the British colonial administration deemed necessary to control black people.

In response, these workers entered the political arena, becoming Kenya's first nationalistic group.

The political activity of black Kenyans spread out from Central province in the 1920s and 1930s. Most prominent of the Kenyan political organizations before World War II was the Kikuyu Central Association, which was formed in 1925. Jomo Kenyatta (then known as Johnston Kamau) became its general secretary in 1928. In 1929 Kenyatta went to Great Britain to petition the British government for elected black representation on the Legislative Council, but the petition was ignored. It was not until 1944 that the first black Kenyan was nominated to the Legislative Council.

In 1946 Jomo Kenyatta—who had been attending a university in Britain since 1931—returned to Kenya and assumed leadership of the newly formed Kenya African Union (KAU). This group put demands based on ethnic, economic, and political equality before the British government, but all were refused.

During the Mau Mau uprisings of the early 1950s, the British colonial government detained or imprisoned Africans suspected or known to be involved in the rebellious movement.

Independent Picture Service

Mid-Century Uprisings

From 1948 to 1950 discontent smoldered among all Kenyans, but particularly among blacks. Since their negotiations with the British government were unsuccessful, black Kenyans turned to secret political societies—one of which became known as the Mau Mau. Committing acts of violence, some secret societies directed their frustrations toward the Europeans and the colonial government. The terrorists' goal was to keep the colonial government off balance and to prevent whites in Kenya from gaining independence from Britain—that is, independence without equal political rights for black Kenyans.

The terrorist activities increased in number and violence, reaching riot proportions. In October 1952 the British colonial governor declared a state of emergency, and all black Kenyan political parties were outlawed in 1953. Lumped together by the British government under the name Mau Mau, the secret societies were believed to be linked to the KAU.

Many restrictions were placed on black Kenyans during the state of emergency, and often people fled to the forests to avoid confrontations with the police. Police rounded up hundreds of black Kenyan political leaders and hasty trials were held, after which most of the important political leaders—including Jomo Kenyatta—were imprisoned in 1953. In the meantime, the

Housing estates built by the government improve living standards for many Kenyans. The Kikuyu discovered the economic advantages of village life when the British colonial government moved them from their family homesteads during the Mau Mau rebellion. Many chose to remain in the government settlements after the crisis.

Independent Picture Service

Asians, who worshipped in mosques such as the one shown above, received political representation in the colonial government in the 1920s—two decades before Africans did. Non-Africans now make up less than 1 percent of the population in Kenya and live primarily in large cities.

secret societies attempted to keep the spirit of rebellion alive while their leaders were in jail. Although the state of emergency lasted through 1960, most of the terrorist activity of the Mau Mau and the resulting British retaliations occurred between 1952 and 1955.

The Road to Independence

Beginning in the late 1950s, other ethnic groups joined the Kikuyu to demand black Kenyan rule. In June 1955 the ban on political parties was lifted—excluding the parties of the Kikuyu—and many small, ethnically based parties were formed. The Kenya African National Union (KANU), which was the party most similar to the KAU, became the largest of these. Its main rival party, the Kenya African Democratic Union (KADU), also became quite powerful. The unifying element of these

When Kenya achieved self-government in 1963, Jomo Kenyatta—the independent nation's first chief executive—pledged that the country would release itself from all foreign domination.

33

parties was the desire for the release of Jomo Kenyatta. The groups also wanted a general election for black Kenyan representatives to the Legislative Council.

In the late 1950s Kenyan politicians also faced the problem of whether to push for independence as well as for majority (black Kenyan) rule. By 1959 political activism made it obvious to the British government that Kenyans would settle for nothing less than independence with majority rule. This meant the majority of seats in the legislature would have to be held by black Kenyans because they made up the largest segment of the population. In January 1960 a constitutional conference was held in Britain that established majority rule as the basic principle of the forthcoming Kenyan constitution.

Finally, in February 1961, elections were held to choose black Kenyan representatives for a new parliament. The KANU party won the elections, but its representatives refused to take office until Jomo Kenyatta—the acknowledged party leader —was released from prison. But the British did not meet this demand until August 1961, and in the meantime the rival KADU party formed a government. Nevertheless, Kenyatta's eventual release ensured British cooperation in Kenya's independence.

Building a Nation

Declaring their independence from Great Britain on December 12, 1963, Kenyans elected the KANU party to choose a governmental system for the new nation. Jomo Kenyatta became Kenya's first prime minister. The following year Kenya became a republic with Kenyatta as its president. In the same year, the minority KADU party—which had been formed by several small ethnic groups that feared domination by the large groups of Kikuyu and Luo—joined the KANU party. Since then Kenya has operated essentially as a one-party state, although it permits considerable freedom within the party.

Under Kenyatta, the government immediately began to replace the colonial economic and cultural systems. The government took over farms and businesses held by Europeans who had not become

Artwork by Jim Simondet

Kenya's coat of arms, which bears the motto *harambee* (pull together), depicts Mount Kenya covered with coffee, tea, maize, and sisal. Two lions stand on top of the mountain holding a Masai shield, which carries the symbol of the KANU party—a rooster with an axe.

Artwork by Jim Simondet

Kenya's national flag features a Masai war shield and two crossed spears, symbolizing the defense of freedom. In the background, the black stripe represents the African population; red stands for their blood and the struggle for freedom; and green is a symbol of the rich land. Two white stripes represent peace and unity.

Courtesy of Eliot Elisofon, Elisofon Archives, National Museum of African Art, Smithsonian Institution

Former president Jomo Kenyatta inspects military guards in Mombasa.

Kenyan citizens and sold or rented these properties to black Kenyans. Both public and private education were expanded. Kenyatta also succeeded in increasing national pride among people who historically had more loyalty to their individual ethnic groups than to the national government.

Kenyatta died in 1978 at the age of 86. He had governed Kenya from the time of independence until the time of his death. Vice president Daniel T. arap Moi became Kenyatta's successor and continued the moderate economic policies begun by Kenyatta. The nation's politics, however, have come to be dominated by a few powerful Kenyans. This situation has encouraged corruption and has aggravated ethnic tensions. After a failed coup in 1982, the government cracked down on dissent. Subsequent charges of human rights abuses have strained Kenya's relations with the international community.

Although the nation has in effect been a one-party state since the 1960s, the constitution was amended in 1982 to make the KANU party the only legal political party. In 1986 another change to the constitu-

Independent Picture Service

The legislature meets to make decisions in Nairobi's Parliament Building *(above)*, which bears the crest of the Republic of Kenya. The KANU is the only legal political party in the country, and unity is emphasized at all levels. Schools *(below)* stress the importance of national identity.

Independent Picture Service

Photo by UPI/Bettmann Newsphotos

President Moi *(left)* met with U.S. president Ronald Reagan in March 1987.

tion eliminated the secret ballot in primary elections. Voters now have to line up publicly in support of their candidate.

In February 1988 President Moi was elected to a third five-year term. Challenges to his government's authority continue to arise, however. Since 1986 teachers, students, journalists, and other dissenters have been imprisoned in connection with the activities of an opposition group known as Mwakenya.

Government

The Republic of Kenya is run by a president and a national assembly, or parliament. All citizens over the age of 18 are eligible to vote for the president, who is elected to a five-year term. The president exercises strong executive authority and appoints a vice president and cabinet ministers from the national assembly. Of the members of the national assembly, 158 are elected by popular vote to five-year terms and 12 are appointed by the president.

The high court of Kenya directs the judicial branch of the Kenyan government with a chief justice and at least 11 associate judges, all of whom are appointed by the president. District courts rule on local issues.

The seven provinces of Kenya are divided into 40 districts that administer local government. Each district has its own commissioner, who is selected by the president. Commissioners raise funds for the local concerns of their districts, such as education, public health, transportation, and self-help projects. Although these local political units are responsible to the national government, they exercise considerable freedom.

The constitution of the Republic of Kenya establishes a strong role for local government. During the initial years of independence, weekly town meetings were an important communication link between the national government and the population. At the meetings, community leaders discussed new government policies, held local trials, and oversaw decision making.

A woman distributes the weight of a gourd by suspending it by a strap from her head. Gourds are often used for transporting water, since piped water is unavailable to most Africans.

3) The People

Kenya is a nation of more than 30 ethnic groups with different languages and customs. One of the most difficult tasks facing the new republic is achieving unity among these diverse peoples. The nation's motto, harambee—"pull together"—was introduced by Kenyatta to unite Kenyans psychologically as well as economically and politically. Of the nation's 23.3 million people, only 1 percent are non-African, including those of south Asian and European descent. Most of these minorities live in cities and towns, whereas only 1 in 20 black Kenyans reside in urban areas.

Kiswahili and English are the official languages in Kenya, and Kiswahili serves as the language of commerce among many ethnic groups. A Bantu tongue that uses many Arabic words, Kiswahili developed during the Arab domination of the East African coast, where it is still widely spoken. Farther north, especially around Nairobi and other large cities, English is widely used.

At Kipsain, a Kalenjin girl carries a younger member of her family. It is common for boys to tend cattle and for girls to babysit when they are quite young.

Ethnic Groups

Various attempts have been made to categorize the many ethnic groups that compose Kenya's population. A great variety of languages and customs has arisen from historical movements of peoples in East Africa during the past 2,000 years. Many historians and linguists (those who study language) have noted similarities among these different peoples based on their languages. Four major language groups are represented in Kenya's African population. Some ethnic groups, such as the Kikuyu and the Luo, have assimilated Western culture almost completely. Other groups, like the Masai and the Boran, have sought to retain their own practices and dress.

BANTU-SPEAKING PEOPLES

The Bantu-speakers form the largest linguistic group in Kenya, comprising about 58.5 percent of the population. These peoples originally inhabited three distinct regions of the country—the upper area of Lake Victoria, central Kenya, and the extreme southern portion of the coast. Although all Bantu-speaking peoples have similar customs, there are several subgroups included in this category. The largest single Bantu-speaking group in Kenya is the Kikuyu, who comprise roughly 21 percent of the population. Other important Bantu-speaking groups are the Luhya, who make up 14 percent; the Kamba, who number just over 11 percent; and 5 percent who call themselves Meru.

NILOTIC PEOPLES

Kenya's Nilotic peoples are named after their original location in Sudan near the Nile River. The main Nilotic group in Kenya is the Luo, the third largest ethnic group in the country—after the Kikuyu and the Luhya—making up over 13 percent of the population. Since migrating to Kenya, the Luo have inhabited the area around Lake Victoria and its southern boundaries.

Other Nilotic peoples are concentrated in the Rift Valley of western Kenya, where

Independent Picture Service   Independent Picture Service

Wearing ornaments made from beads and iron, a Kuria girl (left) waits her turn to dance in a ceremony. The Kuria people, who historically lived in the Machakos and Kitui area, were wood-carvers and ironsmiths. A Luo elder (right) lives in southern Nyanza province, near Lake Victoria. Ethnic groups are distinguishable not only by their differing customs and clothing but also by physical characteristics, such as height and coloring.

Flutes, such as the one being played by this Pokot man, may be made of bamboo, sorghum, or other hollow plants. Ancient stories and songs are kept alive by the folk music of nearly every ethnic group.

Photo by Phil Porter

Independent Picture Service

These Samburu boys tend their family's cattle. Because the food most Africans eat is basically starchy, some ethnic groups bleed their cows—a practice that does not injure the cattle—to add protein to their diet. The cows' blood is then mixed in a gourd with milk.

the population is divided between Bantu and Nilotic groups. Like the Luo, these peoples descend from groups that originally migrated into present-day Kenya from the north. Sometimes referred to as Kalenjin, these peoples divide themselves into several smaller ethnic groups, but collectively they compose 11 percent of Kenya's population. Historically they have been highland farmers occupying land at elevations of between 5,000 and 8,000 feet.

41

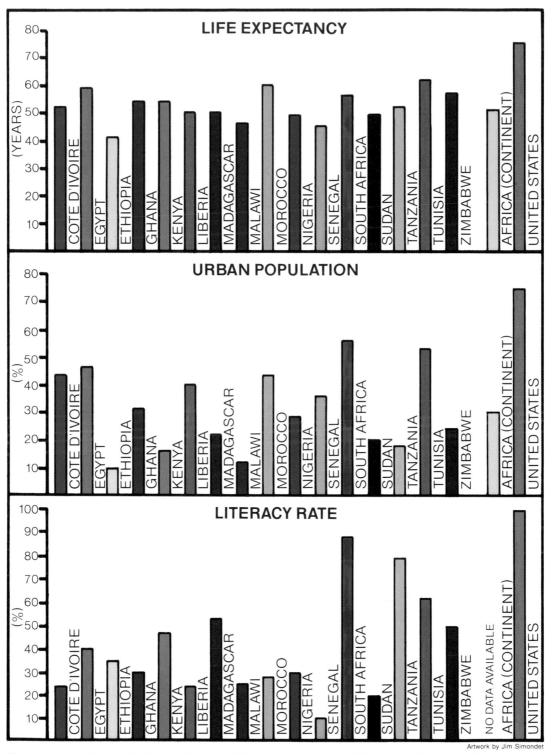

LIFE EXPECTANCY

(YEARS)

COTE D'IVOIRE · EGYPT · ETHIOPIA · GHANA · KENYA · LIBERIA · MADAGASCAR · MALAWI · MOROCCO · NIGERIA · SENEGAL · SOUTH AFRICA · SUDAN · TANZANIA · TUNISIA · ZIMBABWE · AFRICA (CONTINENT) · UNITED STATES

URBAN POPULATION

(%)

COTE D'IVOIRE · EGYPT · ETHIOPIA · GHANA · KENYA · LIBERIA · MADAGASCAR · MALAWI · MOROCCO · NIGERIA · SENEGAL · SOUTH AFRICA · SUDAN · TANZANIA · TUNISIA · ZIMBABWE · AFRICA (CONTINENT) · UNITED STATES

LITERACY RATE

(%)

COTE D'IVOIRE · EGYPT · ETHIOPIA · GHANA · KENYA · LIBERIA · MADAGASCAR · MALAWI · MOROCCO · NIGERIA · SENEGAL · SOUTH AFRICA · SUDAN · TANZANIA · TUNISIA · ZIMBABWE · NO DATA AVAILABLE · AFRICA (CONTINENT) · UNITED STATES

Artwork by Jim Simondet

The three factors depicted in this graph suggest differences in the quality of life among 16 African nations. Averages for the United States and the entire continent of Africa are included for comparison. Data taken from "1987 World Population Data Sheet" and *PC-Globe*.

The Pokot people are a pastoral group from northwestern Kenya. The traditional means of ethnic identification—hairstyles and jewelry—are becoming less popular as a national identity becomes stronger.

Photo by Phil Porter

Courtesy of Minneapolis Public Library and Information Center

Masai girls often have their marriages negotiated for them by their fathers before they are born. As old women, however, they enjoy the same distinguished status that male elders do.

A young Masai experiments with a javelin, laying down his own long-bladed spear. The Masai have resisted absorption by Western culture for centuries and continue their nomadic lifestyle as herders on reserved lands in the south.

The Masai, another Nilotic group, are probably the best-known ethnic group in Kenya, both because British colonists were fascinated by them and because tourism continues to focus on them. The Masai number fewer than 250,000 people, but they are well known because of their romantic reputation as fierce warriors and cattle keepers. The nomadic way of life of the Masai is dying, however, because Kenya's need to feed its growing population has reduced the land available for grazing.

CUSHITIC PEOPLES

Constituting the smallest language group in Kenya, the Cushitic peoples include those who historically inhabited the north and northeast of Kenya. Influenced by Afro-Asiatic languages spoken in northern Africa and the Arabian Peninsula, the Cushitic groups are primarily nomads who herd camels and sheep in Kenya's dry regions. The Galla and other Somali-speaking peoples, as well as the Boran—who form the largest ethnic unit in this area—are representative groups.

In the late nineteenth century, rinderpest—a fever that affects cattle—destroyed African herds. More disease-resistant strains have since been developed, and during the 1980s Kenyans raised more than 12 million head of cattle.

Important social values in Kenya include taking the time for leisurely conversation and, for men, developing lifelong male friendships.

Customs

Most ethnic groups have common customs dealing with family life, marriage, becoming adults, and other practices. These customs vary in degree of ritual but not in importance. The family unit, which embraces those living together in a village—including cousins, nephews, nieces, uncles, and aunts—is extremely important.

Once children begin to earn a living, it is their duty to take care of their parents. No matter where in the country they have found employment, children will send a portion—or, in an emergency, all—of their salary home. This money may be used to help pay for the education of younger children at home or it may go for medical supplies for an ailing relative. Among almost all ethnic groups, the grown children take responsibility for the older people. Elderly people are treated with respect, for it is believed that the years they have lived have made them wise.

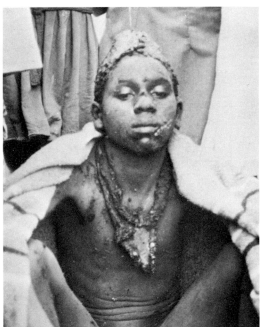

A young Abaluhya boy rests after undergoing a coming-of-age ritual. Because he expressed no pain during the ceremony, he is now considered an adult.

45

Photo by Liba Taylor

Urban and Rural Life

Although life in Kenya's urban areas is fast-paced, village life tends to follow the flow of the seasons. In the cities, many men dress in suits and ties. On festive occasions, such as Independence Day or Kenyatta Day, many African women wear *kangas,* which are long pieces of cloth wrapped around the body. Men often wear loose, collarless shirts (*dashikis*) printed in bright African designs.

In the country, people live a life adapted to the needs of an agricultural economy. Trips to towns often are full-day excursions by *matatu* (local bus), taxi, bicycle, or on foot. In October, when the harvesting is completed, the men take their farm products to the towns in order to sell them. They return with money or articles they have purchased for their homes—such as lamps, blankets, and tools.

When the farm work is completed at the end of each day, the men usually get together to talk, either at someone's house or at *dukas* (small shops). In many parts of the country there is no electricity, and the countryside is dotted with small fires during the evening hours. Whereas wealthy city dwellers can have a nightlife if they choose it, rural residents usually retire early and rise early in the morning.

Although this rural family (above) can take a taxi part of the way home from town, they still have a long way to walk down dirt paths. Nevertheless, technology is changing rural as well as urban life. Large-scale farming is on the rise and uses modern equipment (right).

Courtesy of OPIC

City dwellers enjoy activities that are often unavailable in rural areas. This Kikuyu woman dines at a restaurant in Mombasa.

Courtesy of Sarah J. Hausauer

Courtesy of Stephen Mustoe

Migration to urban areas in response to rural poverty has created a population crisis in Kenya's major cities. Traditionally, an owner's property is divided equally among his children, often resulting in plots that are too small to support families.

Muslims are concentrated along the coast of the Indian Ocean, historically the region of Arab settlement. This mosque—or Muslim place of worship—is located in Mombasa.

Religion

Religious freedom is guaranteed for all Kenyans, and the religious composition of the population is quite varied. Protestants number 38 percent, Roman Catholics represent 28 percent, and supporters of traditional beliefs account for 26 percent. Muslims—followers of Islam—are the least numerous religious group, supported by 6 percent of the population.

Many of Kenya's people have their own ethnic religious practices. Others have adopted Christianity and are church members. Many customs of the African population of Kenya have survived within the framework of the Christian churches without conflict. Polygamy—the practice of having more than one wife—however, has caused some strain between the people of Kenya and the Christian churches. It has long been an African custom for a man to take as many wives as he can afford to

support. In this way, the family continues to grow as the marriages produce many children who will help support the family when they are adults. Christian missionaries felt that this practice conflicted with their beliefs.

Nevertheless, the Christian religion has played a big role in the development of Kenya, and the churches are still growing. Muslims are found mostly along the coastal region. A small percentage of Hindus of East Indian ancestry worship in temples in cities and towns throughout the country.

More than one-quarter of Kenyans are Roman Catholics, who may attend churches like this one in Mombasa. Kenya's Catholics often blend Church teaching with traditional customs.

Sports and Recreation

Recreational activities and sports are an important part of life in Kenya. The most popular athletic activities are soccer, track and field, cricket, and water sports. Athletes are encouraged in both school sports and local and nationwide competition. Kenyans demonstrate particular ability in distance running. Kipchoge Keino, who won Olympic gold medals in 1968 and 1972, and Henry Rono, who held four world athletic records during the 1970s, are two of Kenya's best-known runners.

Soccer is the national team sport, and Kenyan teams play many international matches with teams from Great Britain, West Germany, and Eastern Europe, as well as with other African nations. Schools sponsor soccer teams, and a nationwide league has teams representing the cities and towns of Kenya.

In addition to sports, dancing has always been a popular recreational activity.

Courtesy of Sarah J. Hausauer

Although many who live inland may never see the Indian Ocean, Kenyans who live along the coast take full advantage of the chance to swim and snorkel.

Both ethnic dances and dances introduced by the Europeans are well known. For people living in cities and towns, dancing and attending movies are popular means of relaxation.

Courtesy of Stephen Mustoe

Kenyans are often strong runners, as these competitors in a 5,000-meter (3.1-mile) footrace near Kaptagat demonstrate. Kipchoge Keino and Henry Rono are recent Kenyan running stars who have made names for themselves in international competitions.

49

Two men play a board game called *kigogo*, in which one player tries to take the opponent's playing pieces. Dried beans or round stones are commonly used for the pieces.

Literature

Kenya's literary heritage has been based on oral traditions. Myths, folk tales, and proverbs have been transmitted verbally from one generation to the next and often impart a message or moral. Symbolism—the use of a visible sign to represent something invisible, such as happiness, anger, or sadness—is an important element in this tradition. Common topics include religion, history, nature, and everyday life. Because of the long-practiced custom of storytelling, speech is considered a form of artistic expression, and those who speak well are highly respected.

The oldest form of written literature is Kiswahili poetry and prose from the coastal areas. Prose writing was used primarily to record historical, religious, and legal matters. Initially, most of the poetry was

Courtesy of Tom O'Toole

Although English is Kenya's official language, Kiswahili is equally common and often appears on bilingual road signs.

recited or sung. Only later, after gaining public approval, were poems written down. Different kinds of poems follow distinct forms. For example, *mashairi* (improvised minstrel songs) traditionally have two-line stanzas, or sections, with each line containing either 12 or 20 syllables. *Tenzi* (educational poems) are composed of four-line stanzas—sometimes over 1,000 stanzas long—about subjects such as bravery, romance, history, and religion.

Recent cultural activities in Kenya have been closely connected with politics. The rise of the independence movement, for example, encouraged nationalist literature. The most famous work from this period is Jomo Kenyatta's *Facing Mount Kenya*, which depicts the life of the Kikuyu.

Since independence, writers have revealed some of the inequities in their society. The contemporary works of Ngugi wa Thiong'o best illustrate this point. Ngugi's novels—*Weep Not Child*, *The River Between*, *A Grain of Wheat*, and *Petals of Blood*—move from anticolonial themes to those of economic injustice since independence. His later works in Kikuyu—a language more accessible to poor people

—speak so directly about unfairness and corruption among the elite that they were banned. Ngugi is now in exile after having been detained by the Kenyan authorities as a potential threat to political stability.

Education

An important aspect of life in Kenya is the concern that the government shows for education and welfare. The largest single expense in the Kenyan annual budget is for education. The government provides free primary schooling, although attendance is not compulsory. About 83 percent of children between the ages of 6 and 12 go to primary school, and many above the age of 12 also attend classes. In the 1980s, however, only about half of the nation's people were literate.

In the past, elders within each ethnic

Courtesy of Stephen Mustoe

These boys work math problems at a school in Kitany, near Kaptagat. Patterned after the rigorous British model, the school system in Kenya requires students to pass difficult standardized exams before continuing to the next grade level.

community gave children a practical education. For example, children were taught ethical principles, the history of their people, and useful information on farming and cattle raising. Kenya is now undertaking a vast development scheme to replace the old style of education, because it does not provide people with the skills needed to increase industrialization and economic development.

Kenya's educational structure was originally modeled after the British system, with seven years of primary school and six years of secondary school. In 1985 Kenya changed its system to eight years of primary school, four years of secondary school, and four years of university-level education.

Students who complete the primary level must take an examination to determine whether they can go on to secondary school. After completing the four-year secondary program, students take another examination for entry into a university-level program. Kenya has two universities—the University of Nairobi and the new Moi University in Eldoret—both of which are controlled by the Ministry of Education.

Because most Kenyans do not attend school beyond the primary level, courses that teach children skills they will use to make a living are the most valuable. Pupils at a boys' school *(left)* learn farming techniques, and a teacher at a rural classroom in the Kerio River Valley *(below)* works to improve the nation's 50-percent literacy rate.

Independent Picture Service

Courtesy of Stephen Mustoe

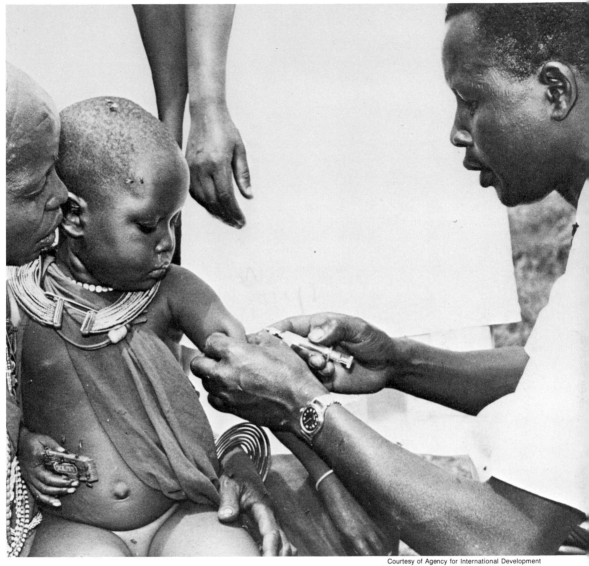

A Masai child receives an inoculation against disease. Most rural communities cannot support a permanent clinic, and patients must wait to receive treatment from traveling medical personnel.

Health

The government has made improved health care for Kenyans a high-priority project. Almost everywhere in the young nation there is a growing respect for preventive medicine (practices that seek to prevent the development of health problems). Government health agencies are attempting to wipe out the conditions that cause malaria and sleeping sickness, as well as to educate Kenyans about health and sanitation.

Modern hospitals are found in the cities and towns, and in the rural areas there are dispensaries—which supply medical and dental care—mission hospitals, and clinics.

53

Kenya's struggle to provide adequate food, shelter, education, and health facilities for its population becomes still more difficult as the population figure skyrockets. Government efforts to limit the average family size meet with resistance from traditionalists.

Courtesy of Tom O'Toole

Photo by Phil Porter

Agriculture is a crucial factor in the future of Kenya's people. It will determine their health, their jobs, and where and how they will live. Erosion of the land is one threat to food production that Kenya cannot ignore.

The life expectancy in Kenya is 54 years of age. Although this figure is slightly higher than the average of 51 for East Africa, it is well below the average of 74 for industrialized countries.

Kenya is facing a serious health problem with the spread of AIDS (acquired immune deficiency syndrome). As of March 1987, 286 cases of AIDS had been reported in Kenya, and the virus is expected to reach epidemic proportions in the next decade. Educational and medical programs to prevent the spread of AIDS are needed. Developing and running these programs will require assistance from the international community, since Kenya lacks the funds and the scientific tools to carry out an effective, long-term program by itself.

Another major problem facing Kenya is a 4.1 percent annual rate of population growth—one of the highest in the world. This means that Kenya's current population of 23.3 million will double by the year 2005. Food requirements will also double, but agricultural production will not be able to meet the demand. In an attempt to lower the growth rate, international agencies have increased their contributions for family planning programs in Kenya. Traditional values, however, keep many Kenyans from participating in these programs.

Photo by Liba Taylor

This family is proud to have their own cows. For many Kenyans, fresh milk is hard to obtain.

4) The Economy

Under President Moi's direction, the government of Kenya has encouraged foreign investment and the development of the private sector of the economy. It has also carried out reforms to reduce prices. The country nevertheless faces economic problems, which were made worse by the drought in 1984.

The nation's debts far outweigh its income, and the costs of staple foods continue to rise despite government efforts to curb the increases. In addition, widespread unemployment and a shortage of consumer goods create daily hardships for many Ke-

nyans. Per capita income, the average yearly earnings per person, stood at $309 in the mid-1980s—a figure well below the average for African countries. Kenya's wealthy few have done quite well, however, and corruption among officials remains a drain on the economy.

Agriculture

Throughout its history, Kenya has been predominantly an agricultural nation. As a result, its economy is subject to the uncontrollable forces of the weather. Drought

Courtesy of Stephen Mustoe

This farm, or *shamba,* near Kaptagat demonstrates how to grow many crops at once, rather than relying on a single product. In this way, if one crop fails, farmers still have several more with which to support themselves.

Courtesy of OPIC

Cash crops are raised to sell to someone else. Cattle *(above),* for example, are usually raised for export. Subsistence crops, on the other hand, are grown to feed the farmer's family. Cabbage *(below)* has been harvested and bagged at a local farm.

Courtesy of Stephen Mustoe

and floods periodically have a disastrous effect on Kenya's economy and on the standard of living for the nation's people. Although attempts have been made in recent years to introduce light industry, Kenya remains mostly a land of farmers.

Two kinds of farming are practiced extensively—subsistence farming and cash-crop farming. The difference between the two is basically economic. Subsistence farming means growing only enough crops to feed a farmer's family; cash-crop farming means growing a certain product that is eventually sold for profit. Some farmers combine the two types of farming, but the majority are subsistence farmers.

56

The subsistence farmers of Kenya grow maize (corn), millet, rice, sweet potatoes, cassava (a starchy root crop), bananas, potatoes, coconuts, and pineapples. Maize is probably the most widely grown crop in Kenya because it is the primary ingredient in the staple of the Kenyan diet, a stiff cornmeal dough called *ugali*.

The government is trying to increase cash-crop production to balance the value of its exports with the value of its imports. Government officials hope that the growing of cash crops will eventually replace subsistence farming. The principal cash crops for export are coffee, tea, sugarcane, maize, wheat, sisal (a fibrous plant used to make rope), pyrethrum (a natural insecticide), and cotton. Pineapples and coconuts are grown for both export and local consumption.

For many years coffee beans were Kenya's leading export, but problems in the world markets have caused a fall in the price of coffee. Although the beans are still being grown extensively in Kenya, lower world coffee prices have led to an expansion of tea growing. Kenya's tea is of a high quality and is popular on the Eu-

Farmers in Western province exchange ideas about current planting procedures and about the most valuable crops to grow. Maize, growing in the field behind the group, is the most important food crop in Kenya.

Mechanized agriculture has been expanding in Kenya since colonial days, transforming tasks that used to require days to complete into jobs that now take a matter of hours.

ropean market, especially in Great Britain. Although the severe drought of 1984 caused Kenyan coffee production to fall in a single year to 97,000 tons from a high of 130,000 tons, production has improved since 1985. Tea production has surged despite the drought, reaching approximately 147,000 tons.

Pyrethrum, another important cash crop, grows best in the highlands at elevations of 6,000 to 8,000 feet above sea level. The leaves and daisylike flower of this plant are used in making insecticides. Kenya's pyrethrum farms are valuable to the country's export trade, ranking high as a source of foreign income. Finally, some maize is exported to other parts of East Africa, and these sales also bring cash into the country. After 1980 agricultural output grew at a rate of 2.6 percent, which represented a slower growth than had been experienced in previous years. During the drought of 1984 agricultural production dropped by 3.7 percent.

57

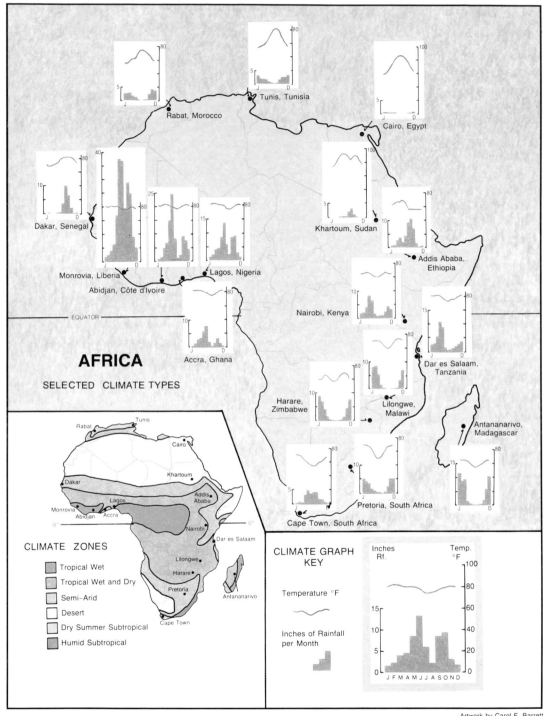

AFRICA

SELECTED CLIMATE TYPES

Rabat, Morocco

Tunis, Tunisia

Cairo, Egypt

Dakar, Senegal

Monrovia, Liberia

Abidjan, Côte d'Ivoire

Lagos, Nigeria

Khartoum, Sudan

Addis Ababa, Ethiopia

Accra, Ghana

EQUATOR

Nairobi, Kenya

Dar es Salaam, Tanzania

Harare, Zimbabwe

Lilongwe, Malawi

Antananarivo, Madagascar

Pretoria, South Africa

Cape Town, South Africa

CLIMATE ZONES

Rabat
Tunis
Cairo
Khartoum
Dakar
Addis Ababa
Lagos
Monrovia
Abidjan Accra
Nairobi
Dar es Salaam
Lilongwe
Harare
Pretoria
Antananarivo
Cape Town

0°   0°

- Tropical Wet
- Tropical Wet and Dry
- Semi-Arid
- Desert
- Dry Summer Subtropical
- Humid Subtropical

CLIMATE GRAPH KEY

Inches
Rf.

Temp.
°F

Temperature °F

Inches of Rainfall
per Month

J F M A M J J A S O N D

Artwork by Carol F. Barrett

These climate graphs show the monthly change in the average rainfall received and in the average temperature from January to December for the capital cities of 16 African nations. On the graph for Nairobi, Kenya, the monthly temperatures are relatively low, even though the capital is very close to the equator. This situation occurs because the high altitude of the city causes lower temperatures. Data taken from *World-Climates* by Willy Rudloff, Stuttgart, 1981.

A mash made from maize flour and water, *ugali* is a daily feature of many Kenyan diets.

Tourism

Tourism continues to be stressed by the government as Kenya's most important source of foreign currency. Package tours to beach areas have helped to boost the tourist industry in Kenya, which in 1987 welcomed more than 600,000 visitors to the country. Traditionally, the main attraction to Kenya has been game watching and animal photography, but beach holidays are now as popular as safari tours.

Once famous as a place for hunting big game, Kenya now encourages tourists to shoot only pictures of the animals. In recent years, conservation of wildlife, some of whose numbers have dropped alarmingly, has become a major concern.

Of Kenya's several dozen national parks and reserves, some of the most famous are Nairobi, Amboseli, Meru, Tsavo, Mount Kenya, and Aberdare. Improvements have been made in the roads leading to these isolated parks. Each park specializes in some particular type of wildlife, and a tourist could spend several weeks visiting all of them. For viewing elephants, Tsavo

Safaris, or trips through the African wilderness, are still very popular with tourists. Here, a vervet monkey inspects a car parked in Nairobi National Park.

59

Courtesy of Stephen Mustoe

The island of Lamu is becoming an important tourist attraction for Kenya because of the richness of its predominantly Arabic culture, characterized by the dhow — a traditional Arabian sailboat.

National Park is probably the best spot in Kenya; lions are seen to best advantage in the Masai Mara Game Reserve. Other parks have an abundant supply of wildebeests, warthogs, baboons, gazelles, impalas, and various types of birdlife. Lake Nakuru offers tourists a bird sanctuary where flamingos and ibis can be photographed.

Manufacturing

Kenya is one of the most industrially developed countries in East Africa. The manufacturing industry accounts for 15.8 percent of the gross domestic product and employs at least 14 percent of the work force. Since the country achieved independence, the government has invested heavily in industrial development, and foreign countries such as the United States and Great Britain have also contributed to Kenya's industrial growth. Important industries include those that produce or process petroleum, textiles, clothing, cement, meat, food, beverages, dairy products, electrical equipment, motor vehicles, and chemicals.

Transportation

With one of the best transportation systems in Africa, Kenyans depend on trains, boats, and automobiles to get around the country. Of about 1,300 miles of track operated by the Kenya Railways Corpora-

Independent Picture Service

Products from factories owned and operated by the government are much less expensive for Kenyans than they are once they are exported to other markets. These women work in a pineapple cannery in the industrial Thika region near Nairobi.

60

The cement industry thrives in the Bamburi district of Mombasa.

Independent Picture Service

tion, about half of the line serves the area between Mombasa and the Ugandan border. Boats transport both goods and people along the coast and on Lake Victoria, where steamers serve the various East African lake ports, including Kisumu, Kenya's busy inland port. Kenya has about 33,700 miles of roads, but only about 12 percent of them are paved.

Since achieving independence, Kenya has constructed feeder roads, which link agricultural areas to the main roads. In ad-

dition, international roads link Kenya with the neighboring countries of Somalia, Tanzania, and Ethiopia. Road transport is a popular way of moving goods in Kenya because it is faster than rail, though it may be more expensive.

Kenya's main paved road runs from Mombasa to Western province, a distance of nearly 600 miles. Roads leading into the main highway are paved up to a point and then are surfaced with a loose sand and pebble mixture called *murram*. In the rainy

Courtesy of Sarah J. Hausauer

The harbor at Kisumu on Lake Victoria is Kenya's busiest inland port and receives boats from Tanzania and Uganda.

Uniformed schoolchildren in Kitany travel to classes in the open-backed truck that serves as their school bus. Durable trucks often are the only vehicles that can travel Kenyan roads.

Rainfall often interrupts overland travel. The historic floods of 1961–1962 forced at least one vehicle off this causeway on the Athi River.

season, these murram roads are often impassable, which delays overland transport. With improved surfacing of such roads, transportation of goods and people by automobile, truck, and matatu (bus) will become more important and will relieve the railways of their heavy burden.

Kenya has launched its own airline, Kenya Airways, which services international as well as domestic routes. Although Kenya Airways has had its share of financial problems, it continues to be one of the best airlines in Africa. At present, Kenya has airports at Mombasa, Nairobi, Malindi, and Kisumu. By 1983 Kenya had two international airports—Jomo Kenyatta International Airport in Nairobi and Moi International Airport in Mombasa.

The Future

Kenya's hope for the future lies in its ability to increase the number of its skilled workers. As the nation develops its industries, a tremendous need exists for people to fill the positions created by this growth.

Educational programs established by the government are providing more trained personnel to fill these jobs. As a result of the government's efforts, enrollment at all levels of the educational ladder has increased dramatically. As more Kenyans are educated, they will eventually help the nation to improve its economy and to increase its standard of living. With the prospect of these advancements and continued ethnic and political stability, Kenyans share a hopeful outlook for the future.

Photo by Phil Porter

Young Kenyans learn both African traditions and Western-style technology. Both influences will help young people to meet the challenges of modernization.

Index